TO MELT THE STARS

Anna Vaught is an English teacher, Creative Writing mentor, teacher, editor and author of several books. Shorter and multi-genre works are widely published in journals, magazines, anthologies and the national press and she has been a columnist for *Mslexia* and *The Bookseller*. Passionate about access and inclusivity in The Arts, she has curated the Curae prize for writer-carers. Anna is currently completing a PhD by Published Works on magical realism and trauma at York St John University.

CONTENTS

ISBN: 978-1-916938-36-6

Cover designed by Aaron Kent

Edited by Roisin Dunnett

Typeset by Aaron Kent

Broken Sleep Books Ltd
PO BOX 102
Llandysul
SA44 9BG

To Melt the Stars

Anna Vaught

Broken Sleep Books

1. ON MEETING THE MAN

Summer, twenty-five-and-a-bit years ago. The Man asked me for directions on a flooded street. I was living and working in Kolkata at the time. November, twenty-five and a bit years ago, I said goodbye to The Man. It seemed like, whatever we thought, it could not work. I was too broken, we lived in different countries and many other things. Twenty-five years ago, I married The Man.

The Mother I will mention in a little while is my late mother who, since she died in my late adolescence, has been (as in life) a peril to me. It was all broken, you see. But it didn't matter then, and it does not now.

So, I went walking. There was a man on the other side of the street, wading through water happily and going in the opposite direction and he called across to her, 'Excuse me, can you tell me the way I could get to the Blue-Sky Café?'

I was startled because he had chosen a sentence with pleasing internal rhymes (though its tetrameter was imperfect) and momentarily thought I might have imagined him. I said, 'Go straight ahead to the corner and you'll see it there.' To have attempted the beckoning symmetry of the metre really would have been a shade too far. Anyway, what I should have said was, 'Turn round and go straight ahead and you'll see it there,' because the man whirled, lost in the watery street. The ability to give inaccurate directions for the simplest of journeys was a point he raised with me later that day when we met on the same side of the street. Still, he followed me (with his own directions), to home, to the funny old house, and came to visit for a while and then never left. Later, we filled it with laughing and hollering, with crying, children, and a host of rescue creatures.

And I told The Man, 'I forgive you for the broken tetrameter.'

And he said, 'Your directions suck and why didn't you just point to the signpost?'

And I said, 'Signposts and I have a difficult history.'

Looking back, it was as if I met him in a story, stumbling across a book by a familiar author in an unfamiliar place: this was, truly, how it was, after the day in the flooded street in Kolkata. The Man had a calm eye; he didn't wake in the night, sitting bolt upright, like I did. He had faith: he had it in the palm of his hand and the heel of his shoe, and I looked at it and saw possibility and I followed him, just as he followed me. Sometimes, we fell over one another and howled as we travelled on. In another city, I watched him go out and imagined what he saw, single and indivisible: this was how it went.

Varanasi, one of the world's oldest inhabited cities. It was not his city, but I sensed he felt at home there. He sat by the river at dawn and a multitude was there, bathing and praying and offering up what they could.

Look at him. Look at how still he is.

How does he do that?

He is exceptional.

The sun hit the water and he watched the multitude quietly, not able to offer a libation, yet content to watch and bless vicariously. He bought tea and set it by my bed. Then, later, mangoes, limes, tomatoes, onions, and some olive oil from an ayurvedic medicine shop so that he could make a salad dressing of sorts. He begged a small hillock of salt; his eyes said he hoped I would be proud of what he had done. On the balcony of the room, the light was dazzling. There, he assembled breakfast for me, and called me out from my room. I sat at ease; he smoothed my hair, put on my hat, and gave me what he had made. We said little as we ate and watched the sun, still in its ascent. The colour of the Ganges changed from white and gold to the more familiar muddy brown. Now, he stood up and told me that, from now on, he would stop running, stop travelling away from and start travelling to a destination. Whenever he put one foot in front of the other, it would be with me. I understood and that was that. There were smiles of complicity.

But still, I told you I was broken.

'Stay with me.'

'I don't know if I can. I am broken. I was never made properly. There is more than one of me.'

'And you think any of that bothers me?'

In the lanes below, the monkeys chattered. They could smell the food he had prepared and were ready to steal. He spoke a prayer. Then he said: 'And again and again, I don't care who you are and if you are more than one,' he said. Then: 'Broken is beautiful, too. Don't you know that?'

'What about my dead mother? She's still here, all the time, chattering in my ear, telling me how worthless I am, what a little canker I am.'

'We'll ignore her.'

'And The Other?'

'He's fine. He prefers other people to you, so you have an out there.'

'I hurt myself.'

'I'll stanch the blood or maybe just tie you up to stop you doing it.'

'That sounds alluring,' said I. Then, 'What about God who is – Dead if He ever Existed?'

And The Man said, 'He is alive. He was down by the river.'

May I offer a digression?

When he was ten, The Man happened to be in an elevator in a

hotel in Dallas, Texas. In walked a tall man; the boy looked at the man's shoes. From there, it was a long way up, but look he did. The boy saw that it was Johnny Cash. No, he must be wrong. But hang on, Johnny Cash must have had to ride in an elevator some time, so the boy looked again. He nudged his little brother, 'Curtis, I think it's Johnny Cash.' Maybe the man heard him, maybe not. But he bent low and smiled a warm, wide smile and said, 'Helllllllo boys.'

The child was star-struck and cannot remember if he said hello back. Little brother was possibly unmoved, being too young and green to comprehend that Johnny Cash was not to be seen riding in an elevator with you any day of the week. Cash was, like him, a Southern man. Little links kind of went in deep: faith and difficulty and broken things and joy. And riding in that elevator. I noticed that The Man would listen and feel at home; saw that Cash was flawed, powerful and weak. He had struggled with addiction and the darkest of insecurities. Cash had faith that was angry and brave and music that haunted even when it jangled. In a quiet moment, he picked 'Down There by the Train' with its invocation to meet him if you had travelled the low road; if, broken and sinning, you had passed the same way.[1]

There are times when the puzzles and the headaches just drift away: I met The Man and he had a faith that was flawed and wanting and made sense, now that was like moisture on my parched and callow soul and for a while it washed away my feeling of the absurdity and booted those who created it out of the door. It was temporary, but it was beautiful while it lasted. It was utterly beautiful, and I had the tiniest of notions that one day it would come back. One fine day when golden light breaks through the mist and, as in the song, Judas Iscariot, betrayer of Jesus, carries John Wilkes Booth, assassin of Abraham Lincoln; when rifts are healed and the person who hated you forgives you.

Teardrops fell like summer tempests and I, glimpsing the world through another's eyes, (sometime while listening to Johnny Cash) sensed possibility and found it both gorgeous and painful.

Oh, when The Man followed me first, there was much wailing and gnashing of teeth from both families once everyone began to understand that he might be staying. For issuing from tomorrow, come today and other people, when time is no longer away.

The Mother was there, though dead, inviting them all out, smilingly, winningly, 'Come and see my bitch daughter. Look what she's done now.' I felt it acutely, and it is very difficult to explain this sort of thing to others, as if my life were magical realism, the dead and the living intertwined.

One of the neighbours came out from her house and shrieked, 'What the fuck are you doing marrying your holiday romance?' and there was stony silence from all members of both families, probably for the same reason. The words *shotgun wedding* hung heavy in the air: I was visibly uncouth, a liability of big emotions, with a tendency to curse, an untidy Anglo-Cymric background, two dead parents and The Other, who hated me. In normal families, immediate relatives didn't usually leave the younger ones out in a dark and shadowy wood to be eaten by wolves, and normal people didn't discuss violent and splashing death over tea. Did they?

'It's okay,' laughed The Man. 'My family is entirely dysfunctional, too.'

'What about the way the dead are present all the time? That there's little distinction between who's dead and who's not? In my case, who's real and who's not? The Mother has been dead for ten years, but it hasn't made any difference!'

He just sighed. Then he smiled.

Fuck me, *I love him*. It does not matter what you throw at this

11

man; it does not matter what life throws at him. He is the grey rock when required: your bitterness cannot penetrate and your cant, your rhetoric, heresy, or your devious and self-aggrandising acridity are not going to get in. He is just who he is, He says, I'm just a funny guy. *I'm no oil painting, but I'm doing my best.*

You are waiting for the next bit? HAVE YOU NO ANGST? CAN YOU ADD NOTHING IN THE WAY OF HAND WRINGING? I'm afraid not. Why? Because, with his own fine and personal economy, that is all there is and all you need. He believes in Jesus and living in the moment because that's where grace is, where sense is.

The sleep of The Man is untroubled, while my side of the bed has sheets akimbo and a creased book: it's like two halves of a world of a brain.

Say we meet somewhere in the middle.

2. MARRIAGE - COMPLICATIONS,
WHAT MATTERS

He told me he loved me. That meant he was about to fuck off, but no: The Man went down on one knee, held out a bright diamond and aquamarine engagement ring and said, 'Well how's this for misguided?'

And the figures – the family that had derided me and had been watching outside the first-floor window – were going down the ladder, down, down and in the firmament a star now danced as the glittering ring slipped on the finger and the wolves howled at an unquiet distance. Who were the figures? A dead mother, a shadowy father, others, sometimes it was an individual and sometimes just a mass of caustic disapproval, either way making you shiver and that the ground under your feet was unstable. Quick! We're coming to get you.

Now, we couldn't say the wedding day was the happiest day of our lives but, in retrospect, it was undeniably funny. Miraculously, I did not trip and cut a hole in my train or say the wrong name during the marriage vows. I was frightened about what was going to happen. Would everyone suddenly turn on me? Would they laugh at my dress? Would someone stand up and tell The Man he was making a terrible mistake. I remember my heart racing and trying, desperately, to look at the angels on the wall of the nave; the rich carving on the pulpit.

I thought, 'Not here, not now on my wedding day. Let me not be broken today; *let me feel safe*,' but had no-one to say it to. I tried earnestly to control a terrible gripping panic: sneering folk and screaming head. But there followed a strange sensation: it was the wash of tenderness for my parents I felt, unbidden, from time to time. What it came down to, standing there in my bridal gown being roundly told off by new relatives, was: 'I want The Mother. I want her.'

How could that be? The Mother. What? Her cold, shiny shark-eye looked at me from the darkened nave. She didn't advance to comfort her daughter. *Oh, she was a jagged, pointing monster, but she belonged to me.* That was what I thought, in a flash. 'And maybe, in a way, she thought that I was her and she was me and that was why she hated me: because she loved me and didn't want to. Perhaps she really truly loved me against her will and loathed me for it? How unhappy must she have been? Would today have made her proud NO OF COURSE NOT. And I loved her, and I loved her, and she will never let go of me. I killed her and I want her back and maybe I must kill her again!'

You're not supposed to be thinking dark confused things like this on your wedding day. Thinking dark confused things isn't mentioned in the guides and the bright magazines and the wedding journals. *Pollyana fuck* to that because the point was this: for me, things were broken and striated and yet it – this day of coupling –couldn't be taken away from me. And it couldn't be taken away from The Man. There had been moments of significant beauty and comedy. Uncle Ieuan, recently widowed, had promised to walk up the aisle with me in a gold lamé suit (an unusual suggestion for a Welsh hill farmer). He settled on a gentle tweed with slightly grubby trousers in the end. The Man, he intoned, had met with his approval on sight because, 'You're not a bloody Englishman.' Also, during the hymns, the beautiful Welsh baritone of Uncle Howell had reverberated over the flags of the church floor. These fine Welsh waves echoed unnoticed under Southern feet as the groom's spectacularly divorced parents exchanged cursory glances.

It was incendiary: dark and light in one nave.

It is like life, and it is not one thing.

Dark and light in one nave.

And yet,

It is like life, and it is not one thing.

Dark and light in one nave.

And what mattered, in the end?

That I married him; that's it.

The perfect day was ruptured, contained spite and ugly, wretched things. But now I think that I could not have known that beauty unless it had been shit-mired. I remember a relative saying, 'Silly, silly, both of you crying,' but that's not silly and it's not weakness or spectacle: it is bold and scintillating love driving forward and its joy and size do not care if someone thinks they are foolish. It's bigger than that and the best of us, however we find it or celebrate it.

I take you, The Man, to be The Man, to have and to hold from this day forward, for better for worse, for richer, for poorer, in sickness and in health, to love and to cherish, till death do us part, according to God's holy law. In the presence of God, I make this vow.

Would I do it again in a heartbeat? *Oh yes,* I said, *Oh, I would, and I would.* And one day, though it will not be all pretty, I will write a book for you, my darling. I will write many.

3. ON MOTHER - MOTHER'S DAY, EVERY DAY

Some years ago, I wrote my dead mother a letter. It was poetical but promised murder. She was already dead and hated poetry.

I have had a good deal of mental health problems. A colourful time. I have battled, for as long as I can remember I have been prone to unrelenting dark moods; anxiety has, not infrequently, kept me secluded and apart. Depression, OCD, recurrent nightmares, dissociative episodes; the results of developmental trauma. I have been a chronic self-harmer, tried to control the vagaries of a messy world with routine and ritual, twice tried to take my own life. On the first occasion, The Mother found me but refused to take me to hospital. That was a seminal moment. I was fourteen. I thought, 'Maybe she doesn't understand.' But later I thought, 'Maybe she just wanted me to die?' It was hard to feel safe or loved after that, but then I am not sure that I knew what these things meant, so I describe that feeling only with the benefit of hindsight. As a mother myself, I feel so sad for my child-self because I look at my boys and think, *How could you? All those years*! I need to add, however, that it is not necessary to be a mother to understand that you must care for the child you were: that is where all the ladders start. How you begin to climb up, out and to heal.

In the end, I began to access the help I needed. I had CAT (Cognitive Analytic Therapy) on the NHS. It began to change how I saw myself, my life and my past in profound terms. It had homework. I am a swot, so I liked that. Ah, not easy homework. Letters to the therapist and letters to The Mother and assorted other folk whose influence weighed heavily and unpleasantly on me. CAT helped me to see the world in a brighter, fresher way. To live unladen by enervating memory. To get away from rambunctiously alive but very dead relatives. Writing to The Mother was a part of that. I had some things to say, and I had to make a stand and confine her to my past. I would say I am ninety percent there. More recently, I am having trauma therapy with EMDR[2] because I have flashbacks and recurrent nightmares. It is all an adventure.

The Mother has been dead for nearly thirty years. She might have caused more trouble post-mortem than when she was alive and kicking. I can hear her now, as I write this. A sort of hoarse chuckling. She wouldn't have to use actual words, just a look would do. For a tiny Welsh lady with multiple health problems, she kicked a lot. To me, she was Goliath. But we know what happened to him. To the outside world she was brilliant. She was beautiful; Titian hair and deep blue eyes. She was full of resources and craft; a tub thumper, campaigner. A respected pillar of the community to whom I may owe my own campaigning tendencies. She was too clever for the life in which she found herself and was chronically frustrated. Responsibilities and poor health meant she couldn't get out. I think she swam as best she could through a vast sea of might-have-beens had she not been compromised by a weak heart and the attendant illness. And I was another might-have-been: had I not existed, had she not kept me, the baby who further compromised her physical and emotional reserves. Things might have been different. I believe I became her hate figure, because she needed one: pain drives us to dark places. When she told me how I had weakened her, I believed her. When she told me how everyone thought I was a burden and the bringer of harm, I believed that too.

I think the deathly low moods to which I became accustomed, and against which I periodically lost the will to fight, visited me at an early age because I became convinced, mixed up with earliest memories, that I was a scabrous wound, pick, pick, picked away. A shouldn't-have-been which brought on the ghastly-might-have-beens. I tried to tell her how I felt when I was a little older when she declared, as she often did, that I was a trial and burden to all around me. Then, she pulled my hair and my ear and said, like a whirlwind of curses, '*You* feel? Everything is all about you. You little bitch! You will dance on my grave after you've put me in it.' We were folding sheets to put in the airing cupboard when she said that. It's like it was yesterday, the screeches over the laundry-day diligence. A life replete with incongruity. And there was no-one to tell, for she was a middle-class pillar of the community, of good name and standing. So, it had to be me, didn't it? Here was one of the worst things she would say to me. I find it hard to write this even now:

'Little bitch. Little slut! You will dance on my grave after you have put me in it. And we ALL know what you're like!'

It *must* have been true. She couldn't empathise with me because I was a nasty little eldritch child. Credence of this followed soon, each time. The doorbell rang. It was the vicar: 'Oh Mrs Llewellyn, you were so kind to send flowers to my wife when she was so poorly, and you were so kind to read the closing prayer at Mrs Mobbs's funeral.'

And the phone rang: 'Oh Mrs Llewellyn, you have done so much to change the face of this struggling school. You are an inspiration to all teachers and, in fact, to all members of the community.'

And a letter came from the letter box: 'From Greenham Common: Oh Mrs Llewellyn, it was so kind of you to send us so many cakes and all those beautiful, knitted socks and gloves because we protesters don't half get cold and hungry and it's people like you who keep us going.'

So -

I carved out my name with self-loathing on my skin; hit my head with my fists until the ringing in my ears made me feel a little less alone. It had to be me, me, me because it just had to be. How could it be her? Just look at how marvellous she was! And as a response to stress and anxiety, self-harming stayed for over twenty years. If someone didn't like me, or someone disapproved of me or said the dreaded words, 'Oh we ALL know what you're like', I scratched it on my own skin because those were, for me, prompts for a sort of annihilation. I say, a sort, because there was always more laundry to be done afterwards.

And still I tried to talk to her. I saw her resplendence in others' eyes, so I had to keep trying. I wonder if, after all these years, I am still doing that.

'Mother, I feel so sad!'

Ah, it was all the words of the pitiful, self-indulgent creature. She told me flatly that depression, adolescence or even moods didn't exist. These were phrases invented by those who peddled what she called 'Psychobabble.'

Dealing with Exceptionally difficult Kids. Is your Child a Monster? Strategies to Cope. Are You a Saint who Birthed a Sinner? They were left out like coffee table books. Her anger was palpable but denied. She was too pure, too good to be angry. I was the little canker. When her friends came round, she stuffed the books in the cupboard and put out *Country Living* while she and her harping porcelain doll-faced friends drank tea and compared martyrdoms.

I believe that The Mother was unable to have a strenuous conversation with my father, who was bright but not in her league and possibly not aware that he wasn't, as is the way of men. I used to hear them arguing: 'Books, opera, you never take me anywhere, I am so bored, bored, bored, I am practically dead.' Then my father would go and have a burn. The bonfires he always started when indecision, conflict or any sort of hiatus beckoned. He was a good man, but I don't feel I knew him at all. He was tall and strong and his shoulders like Atlas, but he was weaker than his wife and he would acquiesce when she left a hairball from her daughter on the carpet. He loved her and didn't want to upset her, and he had to get ready for Evensong because he was a lay preacher and had responsibilities.

Mother's Day. I cry. Lacy cards in shops and hearts all over. Special events.

That would have been nice, but you cannot control whether people love you or want you; you can only do your little best. We don't want to hear that, but it is true.

What do I think? I think I miss her every day and I will never stop, and I am so angry about that sometimes I want to explode with rage: how can there be love in there after everything and after the years of shivers and night-wakings that we still endeavour to fix?

Damn.

I learned about determination, persistence, and campaigning from her. I don't know whether she believed we had a soul, but she believed in intellect: in using it, deploying it, allowing it to take flight and to animate us. I think she was brilliant. I imbibed so much from her; I feel such sympathy for her because her life could have been so different. I think illness turned to spite and I was an unplanned child she had the heart and gall to keep. I wonder if she had vicarious hopes for me: that I would do the things she wouldn't be able to and yet that was wound up with her own bitterness. Perhaps, as adults, we could have resolved this and got along, healed and communing. I will never know. Not to have had a friendship with her as an adult upsets me, still. Because, despite everything, we had potential.

Did she love me? I think in her own way. Did she want me? I think she hadn't, but loved me, at least sometimes, against her will and grew to hate me too. The last time I saw her, she had been refusing to speak to me for days. I didn't know why. She wouldn't say. That was the punishment. I saw her on a railway platform. I was still waving when she turned away. I never saw her again and I thought that if I saw her dead body I would die too. Yes, I loved her with passion. She loved with spite and flame. It was complicated. Part of me hated her because each day brought with it a fresh knowledge of what a trial and a burden I had been, of the baby that should never have been and who had better atone for having been allowed to survive. I internalised that and I can feel tears pricking my eyes and that my fingers are clammy with a little anxiety as I write this. The hoarse chuckling is there, just at my back.

Now, I have three boys of my own to mother; I do my best; I try; I fail; I try again; I 'fail better' as Samuel Beckett's phrase has it.[3] Sometimes, I even succeed. I'd be lying if I said my experiences of parenting don't regularly evoke the melancholy of being parented myself. But at least now, I have the wherewithal to challenge that brooding, the depression, the OCD which I developed as an attempt to manipulate a bewildering world and hold it in my hand with ritual, order and lines. I am more able to answer back to the anxiety; the self-loathing and self-harming and the times I tried to destroy my own life, horribly propelled by a fiery sense that I should not be. I would have to say that it began with her.

Ah, but there's more to it than that. I've forgiven her, written the letter to her as part of the Cognitive Analytic Therapy a hugely skilled team laid on for me. And I put it all down and consigned her to my past. I feel so sorry that she despised hope for the lie it gave her, but I don't want her to visit, and she had to go. But love is a many-winged creature and in my letter, I also wrote this, it's pathetic; I know it is. I know: 'And you were my jagged pointing monster, but I loved you Mother. I loved you. I couldn't help it. I still love you. And I want you. And I miss you every day and I will never stop.'

And there: love. Incandescent, painful. Loving someone who did so much damage and cursed you and made you this small. I know it does not make sense and anyone reading this with sense all compact and their mother doting on them, will find it horrifying. But human beings are complicated and so I have made the choice to raise things up from those ruins. Dirty, embarrassing love, admiration, and raw hatred in a ball. I cannot make it less complicated.

I *will* not.

I have survived it through words and because I have described it, so I will continue to survive, until I die and if I see her again – which I also hope I will not – I hope only that she is happy and that, in some part of her, she can say sorry because I have atoned enough for being her child.

4. ON NOT BEING MOTHERED, MOTHERING MYSELF, AND ON PREGNANCY LOSS.

I was a strange little girl; whether this was caused by early loss or would have been the same if I had been wrapped in love, impossible to say. I want to say to you, reader, that there is nothing wrong, whatever society seems to impress upon us, with being strange; a weird thing: a curiosity.

'I think,' I wrote to The Mother in a letter for therapy homework, 'that I am either very weird or very clever, Mummy. Maybe I am both. I think that I see and smell and feel things that others do not. I don't mean like they're right there but it's as if they brush the corner of my arm, or something. I don't get on with the other girls at my new school. But then I have all my books and the little collections I make. I sometimes feel that I am making a museum in my bedroom. I have a little table and make piles of books on the floor so that I can feel shelves or parts of shelves with the things I find and sometimes buy because there is the strange antique shop in the high street and at the back are cheaper things, boxes and boxes of tarnished spoons and pill boxes. Then, I put them with a magpie feather and an agapanthus head, a gall, little skeletons and the skin of a snake, a dead cockroach, purple and shiny in the right light.'

As I wrote, I regressed, and I was that little girl again.

She said, 'Be like the other girls, stupid.'

Would you like to know some more incarnations of child Anna? May I share? Now, in my room there were two essentials: the colour table, an invention of mine; a tiny table with shades of the same colour arranged on it, and the little books containing the rules of the room. The colour table (all set out on a darling little wooden stool later presumed lost as tinder for one of the parental bonfires; my father was always having unnecessary bonfires and I think they were, in part, a product of pain as well as of practicality) became an essential part of the room's structure and hue.

I changed the colour table weekly. It was mine, even if I was a little cuss, fuckwit or a Be Like the Other Girls. A memorable table was the pink one: that included a pair of salmon-pink silk knickers borrowed from my grandmother, a polished stone from a craft shop, a rosy cameo brooch of uncertain provenance, a scallop shell with a rim, the pink ones from a packet of refreshers, a Barbie-pink wafer biscuit, a necklace and – depending on the season – some damask flower petals. I set them all down tenderly and at the last minute added a tiny amaranth-tinged gone-off bottle of perfume that had come from the Avon Lady.

I rearranged the treasures regularly, refreshed them if need be. An important thing was that I formed navigable gaps between them. So that, if you were *really* small, say, you could walk along the little roads between the petals of an aster and the cameo brooch. This was the secret bit: the colour was pleasing to any onlooker, but the order, traced round, and round in the curlicues of a little finger – my own little finger – was the private bit.

'If I were a miniature me, I could spend all day basking on the petal, looking up at the gemstone rock' or,

'I could climb on the pink wafer and jump down, sliding across the pink knickers.'

Such a commanding impulse: to arrange little things in groups and trace a finger round the gaps in between; a microcosm that is intimate and seen only by its author. In childhood, it was the one area where I could say, 'I can be me: make things with my hands! And I didn't knock things over or break things.'

All the items on the table stood still, didn't wobble, knock each other over or fall on the floor at my clumsy feet. In these still hours, everything could be at ease: briefly, I was in control. At such decorous times of arrangement and rearrangement, you couldn't hurt me. Little matter, anyway, if a pink shape fell because I had a drawer of reserves. A lovely little gold clock with cherry blossom painted on its sides and fine enamel face. The clock tied in elegantly with the colour table and rounded off the proportions of the microcosmic world.

`There was a ritual to be observed here, again and again: three little steps by the pink wafer, turn around three times and say the first lines of The Secret Garden four times. '"Chapter one. THERE IS NO ONE LEFT.

When Mary Lennox was sent to Misselthwaite Manor to live with her uncle, everybody said she was the most disagreeable-looking child ever."'

Repeat.

When the table was set, the rituals performed just so, I reduced myself, like Alice, so I could travel its roads and, at other times, I made the Rules of the Room. The rules: nothing complicated there. There were laid out lots of little strictures in very bad spelling which I would struggle to replicate now, all set out and neatly underlined in tiny books I had made. I imagined the room as a world to travel in, so the books were partly a guide: the bed was the island, the wardrobe the ship, the chair was the cave and, *Watch out! Don't touch the floor: mermaids could get nasty.* I had bad dreams about them, with the faces of The Mother and her two harpies, the porcelain doll-faced friends with whom she consorted and who would advise her on suffering the dreadful martyrdom of being mother to such a child. My books contained the rules of the world and the room.

'Friends can come in.'

'Doll-faced people cannot.' (I wrote this because, as a child, I was aware that very beautiful, groomed, or perfect faces could hide murky things.)

'There are jellies and After Eights for tea.'

'The room is only lit with candles.' (Unfortunately, not allowed, by decree of The Mother.)

Also, 'Do not touch the colour table.'

'Do not chew gum.'

'Share things.'

And sometimes, 'Let me be just I and not the two of us.' Or, startlingly, 'I am scared I have killed people.' And 'No Mother allowed in my room.'

The books had blank covers and were stapled together badly, because I was a bit young to be a dab hand with the stapler just yet. I lived in fear of The Mother finding them and so moved them around periodically. Every so often, starting in childhood, and subsequently all through adolescence, I would wake shortly after going to sleep, hot, sweating, and frightened. I would get out of bed and check the arrangement of the colour table and the placing of the miniature rule books: the expression of fear – 'Am I or will I be a murderer?' – haunted me. As a child I was scared that the police would come to the door, and as an adult I fear being caught in the street and criticised, eviscerated, by children and parents. Sometimes, I do not know how I have carried this. It is as if I held terrible guilt and thought it was visible to everyone.

As you might imagine, I did not go into parenthood sturdily. In my amateur analysis, I think that because I relied on my imagination so fiercely, I could not switch it off. Life was an adventure because of that, but the flip side was an ability to imagine and feel, viscerally, chillingly, a terrible thing. Bodies severed and babies desiccated, children on edges and ledges and me too inept to save them.

When you first start trying for a baby, perhaps it doesn't really occur to you that it might not work out. Pregnancy is something that is meant to happen, right? Often, yes. But around one in four pregnancies end. I didn't know this when I was pregnant for the first time, bewildered, unable to comprehend what was going on. It happened again, then again. By this time, I was full of others' advice: I could have told you a thousand horror stories, birth stories, infertility stories. I could have given you plentiful anecdotes.

Here are things not to say:

'Oh, you're probably not psychologically ready to have a baby.'

'Well, you are quite an anxious person, so perhaps that's why you can't carry a baby'.

'I think women these days are too aware of pregnancy and lots of pregnancies were lost in the past, unknowing, because women didn't obsess so much.'

'You could come and babysit for me instead'.

'If you adopt, you'll probably fall pregnant straight away.'

'Let me tell you my blood curdling story about a person I knew...'

'If you think about it, years ago women just expected this to happen and got on with it.' To which my riposte would have been, 'I do see your point, but one of my grandmothers had ten children who survived, but did she talk about the losses she had? Yes: she told me, in her late seventies. She didn't forget. She willed them into memory by talking about them.

Then there was another thing: for me, family was a flexible construct. I did not feel bonded with The Mother. I was confused about what love was and what it did, and people got to do because of it and how come it did not make things better? There's something else that's a taboo subject: that other mother figures in your life go on to carry more importance than the person who birthed you or parented you. I won't elucidate this further now, save to say, that I had other ways I felt I might embrace parenting. But I thought I would try a little longer to have a birth child and then think more if it didn't work out. The Mother had always told me I was a terrible person, and this was widely known, and, despite the press of my rational mind, I sometimes felt this was punishment, the loss. Or that I had been visited and found wanting. I tried to explain it, I remember, but the combination is so strange few people would grasp. But that's okay. We waste much time in trying to be understood and even abiding love does not necessarily come with understanding.

Christ what a mash-up of voices!

I needed psychological help, though. What was pulsing through me was trauma response, unmanaged. Instead, I chose to focus on getting and staying pregnant and hoped I would stay well, while worrying I was not well enough.

After three miscarriages, I was referred for some tests; the results came back with something surprising. I had lupus. I also had what is called a balanced translocation: a picture of my chromosomes showed that part of my sixth chromosome had swapped places with part of my seventeenth. If you inherit this in its 'balanced' form, it won't affect you. You have all the genetic information you need to make you. But when you conceive, well, you know that the pairs of chromosomes are from each parent? One half of a pair from you, one half from him. In my case – and I am simplifying this here – that could mean a baby inheriting my 'balanced form' (therefore being a carrier themselves, but otherwise healthy), or it could mean too much of chromosome seventeen and too little of six, or too much of six and not enough of seventeen. In other words, a partial 'trisomy' (a trisomy is an additional chromosome), or a deletion (a bit missing). One combination showed some recorded cases of extremely life-limited babies; the other combination was thought to be incompatible with life.

I feel bound to say that if you are reading this, as the one in five hundred people diagnosed with a translocation and, by some extraordinary chance are recording the same pattern as me, I urge you to look up details or ask a professional – for example a clinical genetic nurse – to find them for you There may be newer information of which I am unaware. And 'Hello.' I have never met anyone else with a translocation, but now you know who I am. You are not alone. You are also not alone if you managed a translocation, a translocation in its rarest form AND your head was permanently on fire.

This was my lowest point. Lupus, a balanced translocation, and the recommendation of genetic testing in any future pregnancy, which carried with it the slight risk of miscarriage. Christmas. The Man and I felt very alone; I didn't feel like I could tell anyone. Not very festive. But then in the new year came more news: we met a lady I shall call PQ (P and Q are the letters given to the short and long arms of chromosomes). A clinical genetic nurse, she explained that my translocation was even rarer because it was a mosaicism: it wasn't in all my cells. Inside, I was like a kaleidoscope.

It also turned out I didn't have lupus. They mixed up my records with someone else's. I had two further miscarriages; the fifth was further on, but it was termed a 'missed abortion.' That's where – I am speaking frankly, and I hope I don't upset you, dear reader – the foetus dies inside you. I cried, on and off, for some time, until there were no more tears, and my womb was empty.

I got pregnant again. I want to tell you this. PQ came round and armed us with a lot of information. And she said, I will always remember it:

'People with translocations can and do have healthy

babies.' We also learned that, in the operation I had just had, they had identified my quirky cell line. Which way it fell, I didn't ask. The obstetrician said gently, 'Do you want to know the sex of the baby?' We were stunned; I had never used the word 'baby' because it seemed wrong. I felt, because of what had been instilled me that I didn't deserve to use the word. I felt my own mother saying I would be a hopeless mother and here was the proof. All that loss. Also, because of my experience of being a girl to a raging mother, I feared having a daughter.

My heart goes out to those who never know why they don't carry a baby to term. No-one would say to us, 'Yes – this is definitely the reason why you keep miscarrying', but PQ did say, 'This is a likely explanation.' So, you see, for us, it was frightening, but we weren't so much in the dark now. I was still pregnant. Nervous, constantly checking to see if I was bleeding, feeling every twinge. And the obstetrician said, 'Don't put additional pressure on yourself. You can't avoid being nervous after what you've been through. This is how it is now.'

That might not be the right advice for everyone, but it was the right information for me; I couldn't expect pregnancy to be a rosy, romantic time. I never had that experience, but that's no hardship. This pregnancy continued. Testing. More testing. I turned away as hard as I could from the screen. I couldn't bear the thought of seeing. I fainted outside the room and PQ picked me up.

The wait for the cells to be cultured is excruciating, so you crack on.

PQ rang – I am weeping, just weeping, writing this – but she said,

'PQ here, got the results: normal chromosomes. Not inherited your balanced form and do you want to know if it's a boy or a girl?'

Baby.

Baby boy.

I want to say that PQ was the first person to see my new-born baby. She said, 'Oh, oh, oh!' Then she said, because she was a geneticist, 'Now do you believe what the books said about positive outcomes?'

'Oh PQ!' And came the tears like summer tempests. You know, I was unable to say the word, *son*? I tried but was mute. It felt too precious to say, as if naming would invoke some form of divine nemesis and my blessing would be revoked. I said, instead, 'the baby' The Man rehearsed with me. It was important, he said, to say, 'This is my son'. It was an acknowledgement. We cannot say our children will always be safe; there is no life without risk. It is important to face this, grasping fear in one hand and joy in the other and embrace what you are given and embrace – and name – that which you love.

Two years later, I was expecting again. I had miscarried three times in the meantime; it had been sad and difficult. I realise, looking back, that I didn't really talk about it. It's like it never happened. People, as I wrote above, can be rich in anecdotes. Or they are embarrassed because pregnancy loss, for whatever reason, is a taboo subject! But PQ was there again. 'Good news. All clear and no inheritance of the balanced form and do you...'

'Yes.'

'Another boy.'

More tempests.

We had another...son, too. Then another. I am struggling to write this word because the sensations surrounded with it do linger. I had three more miscarriages, gave up but, after a few years, decided to try again. There was a seven-year gap between the second and third boy, but here was PQ again and that is my story. PQ has a family tree in the hospital where she works; our boys are on it. I am on it. The kid who felt she wasn't wanted, an aberration. It's pure gift.

Writing this is, I realise, my way of saying goodbye. Later today, I am going to plant some flowers in our garden: roses. Flowers that will last and foliage that will climb and thrive. I never marked all those times – the eleven *elsewheres* – that didn't. Never knew whether to think of them as babies, souls, as in any way sentient or feeling pain. I will probably never know. But I hope that, if you have experienced loss, what I have written might make you feel less alone, although my story will be different from yours. It may be that my description of so many miscarriages gives you hope, or it may be that you already know you cannot face further loss: this I understand. I think that being a mother – and by whatever means – is not the only way to have a fulfilled and happy life. I think – and I am worrying about whether I have the wording right here; I am not sure I have the right to say what I am about to – that it is one part of one way. And should you try, yet find that it does not happen for you, then what I feel is this: you are not less woman. You are *more* because you had the strength and the love to try and to bear loss. And you are magnificent.

Also, I love you forever, PQ.

And, if this is not too odd, and to my darling husband who swallowed his pain to support me, I love all those tiny lives we lost, that we never knew. They were there and then there were not. They were not nothings. They were ours and may they be home somewhere and safe.

5. ON FRIENDSHIP - THINGS I UNDERSTAND, CASUAL ENCOUNTERS, LOVE AFFAIRS AND SO MUCH MORE.

This is a difficult one for me; friendship can be frightening. Despite all the work I have done I am still nervous about making and maintaining friendships because of the things which rattle around my head. I have this big contradiction inside me because I am an oddity; I am weird. I love weird. It's brilliant and that's what I would say to you. Nonetheless, I am not comfortable with it in my skin because I am fearful of rejection and shame. It all goes back to my early days, I think, with The Mother's finger pointing: *who would believe you*. I remember being mocked in front of people. I never learned the difference between loving teasing and shaming, silencing.

People are messy and complicated. I had always been told I was shy, and thought of myself as shy, thought that I did not like parties, big gatherings, that I was the cat which walked alone. There is nothing wrong with this, of course, so if this is actually you, promise me to *be* you, but also consider whether you have formed your idea of yourself around a kernel of what others *told* about yourself.

My kids have always said, 'How do you know that person?' and I'd be, 'I don't. I just met them.' I am forever falling into conversation with people in shops, on tills, on the phone, with customer service. I mention all of this because I was unable to tell that I was, in fact, a raging extrovert. I had received the message from The Mother that I was ill at ease with others and that they thought I was strange. She had said, repeatedly, that my shyness was weakness and a form of self-indulgence. I believed her.

As I write, as I told you above, I am in trauma therapy, with

EMDR. The therapist pointed out something obvious. I had bounded into the room. She said I was vivacious, and I said, 'Who, me?' throwing myself into a chair. Then I thought: I bounded in and threw myself into a chair. Then I thought: I am wearing a long dress with bright flowers on it, I have a sherbet-lemon-coloured corduroy coat on, my hair is big and unruly, and I am wearing a deep pink lipstick.

I thought, 'I AM vivacious.' This was the point, in middle age, when I suddenly understood I was no shy mouse. Then I thought, 'Oh my God I love big gatherings of people and will talk to everyone there. I love the daily flow of chat and gentle open conversations: it is one of the joys of life. I don't like SOME parties; I feel uncomfortable with SOME groups of people because in those gatherings I have been censored or felt uncomfortable – like the party where I was introduced as the weird one, or another recent one when someone else pigeon-holed me to talk about one of my kids who she'd just seen out and about. The comments were not generous. Mothers, for reasons I cannot understand, can be evil to other mothers.

Where am I going with this and what does it do with love and friendship? I'll tell you. Your therapist is not your friend but does operate from a position of kindness and openness and sometimes it is necessary to state the blindingly obvious because the obverse of that may not have been seen by the client, by the patient, so just point it out.

I have felt a release and greater understanding through working with my therapist. We have revisited places and times when I felt shame and embarrassment and that I deserved it. EMDR helps you to get out of loops, helps you stop the whirring in your amygdala. For me, there's a loosening in the body and, with that, an increased boldness and it feels...it *FEELS* like a suffusion of love and I cannot quite explain it, but I suggest it comes from working with a humane and skilled person, genuinely concerned for the loops I am in, and for me to be fully me, out there, vivid, with lilies in my hair if I want. Gradually, I am becoming more confident in my friendships – not just because of therapy, but it is enormously helpful – and I am excited because I am gaining the confidence to let go and, where things are lasting, to go deeper.

Only today I asked someone I don't know very well to come with tea with me on Sunday and another to have a zoom call with me next week. I was surprised at my audacity, just as I have been at my conversations in shops, service stations, on walks, on buses: I shouldn't have been! It's who I am.

Clearly, I am odd, I'm neurodivergent in a delicate number of hues and I thought I was shy and more socially awkward than I was because I went to the wrong parties. I know that I would like: to keep nurturing and making new friends and to accept that love can grow and sometimes it fades. In 2020, as one of my sons became increasingly ill, I fought for support and as the pandemic began, two of mine left school abruptly with lockdown and things were never the same again, and I was terrified. I will not have been the only one. I thought that I could not make new friendships in my life, having seen so many fade away and so many I could not, with the needs of my family, even begin to maintain.

At the heart of friendship and the love it brings is, I would say, self-love, self-regard. When I look at The Man, he seems to have it in spades; we have touched on this already. Not arrogance, but self-acceptance and equanimity. I love to see that in him, but it does not work to copy it. It has taken me decades to unpick what happened to me over a long period, but it is thrilling to me to consider what might be ahead if I can clear my mind and shake off further things.

Friendships, like all things, flux and may end. I may begin a friendship and feel excited, a pang of the erotic, and a wonder of where it will all go, a bit like being in love. Things may fizzle out or an event occurs like a bucket of water on a kindling flame. I have seen, in someone with whom I hoped to spend more time, a scene of cruelty or disdain which immediately casts a person beyond the pale for me and from which I cannot return. Watched a putative friend flinching at a homeless person, display racism, or show me that they believe only in commodities and judge people by their ability to acquire them. Go ahead and call me judgemental but, to me, there just isn't time and space and there is so much beauty out there. I have found that some friendships, after a long breach, snap back in just like that; a surprise to me. I have also had friendships occur on social media and translate beyond my wildest dreams into real life. Ups and downs, but much caper and quest and it transpires that it starts with me.

With a more solid sense that I can be loved and am worth loving, I'd like to think I can let some things go and embrace many new relationships. I wish that for you, too, reader, or rather, *I wish for what you want and need.*

6. ON INTERGENERATIONAL TRAUMA - COMPLICITY, FLYING MONKEYS AND GREY ROCKS.

I believe that many people keep bad faith with themselves. They were not there, did not notice, did not mean it like that, the other person surely did not mean it like that, please keep the family together, do not disrupt things, family is everything, please do not disrupt things, you must have misunderstood, and have you had a lot of therapy, because this sounds like psychobabble to me.

The complicity is not only that they did not intervene at the time, but that, later, the veracity of one's own experience is silenced or just not addressed. The flying monkeys – this is the language of trauma and family estrangement support groups – are those who enable and empower the person who is causing and sustaining trauma. The grey rock is what you must be when trapped in a situation. Do not react, give off nothing. Allow them nothing to work with. Intergenerational trauma describes the process by which the effects of trauma are passed down between generations; it might occur if a parent experienced abuse as a child or Adverse Childhood Experiences. I have watched it happen and watched it fester because there was no honest conversation to be had. All I have been able to do is work on myself, as I have been showing you. Also, I tell tales. I write them down.

Allow me to tell you about a tale of my own, 'Shadow Babies' Supper', from a collection of short fiction called *Famished*.[4] *It is about dolls. Very large ones.* Giant things with their scratchy hair and their watching, rolling eyes. A small doll is one thing, but a giant doll, several giant dolls, set about in a pristine tableau with their long eyelashes, well now I find that chilling. I have been into several houses, in vastly different places – and you must remember

I have seen some very strange things, including my paternal grandmother's séance room – where the tableau and the tidy truth seem more important than the real pain inside in the house. I have greeted that with horror, yet still tried to understand that, for some of us, it is easy to keep a tableau, neatness, and big fake babies, but not done to speak of truths because they are too painful to admit. So, you see, the dolls that made me shudder are not only their blasted selves, but also an allegory of intergenerational trauma. It is the tableau, set out so prettily with toys, trains and canard truths.

Here is one, in a place where I feel sick at the resentment and pain, sulks, bad faiths and fantasy. Allied to that is being a guest in such a place and knowing that part of your reception is hatred and worry that you are the fool who wants to have it out; to bring things to the surface.

It is a frightening thing.

'*Now, with the creatures nearby and their Keeper wishing harm to us but never, ever expressing so – it's not done; it isn't mannerly, speaking so plainly of bad emotions – my instinct was to take my two small children and pelt out into the night. But where? And I wasn't sure it was an emergency, so how could I run to the kindness of strangers? But I sensed my children felt disgust and annoyance, not fear; they were a comfort to me.*

Now, across a dark sky with its flashes of cruel light, the storm took up more, doors rattled and the Keeper of the House – mother, I supposed, of the bloodless infants; feeder – put the patchwork comforters around them, and against the rattles: 'I don't care for draughts.' But the fire was not lit. Why? Perhaps because you wouldn't want to bother the delicate skin of the dolls, old as time, with hair aeons old, from the old lady who'd breathed her last not far away in The Hollows. She'd rolled over and died in her saggy bed near-bald, because she'd sold her hair to pay for a box and so that some pretty little people could be crowned up right.

I have to go back to this house. Someday soon. The two small boys are big now, but they remember it; the very oddness: the silence of the house. But now I have another one, too: a small child. And I've noticed that the Keeper of the House has, in the prettiest of formal letters, expressed more interest in the littlest one; he is rumoured to be the ps and qs and malleable boy. In bad dreams, I see her tugging at his arm, crooning: 'Come sit. Won't you come to me?' Like I said, I have to go back and have to be sympathetic, but he's not leaving my side for a whispered conversation or to play by the doll tableau. I don't know what fear might take hold or could be murmured. What might be imbibed: spirit or very blood. And none of us knows how hard a bloodless infant can kick when it's strong from getting all the love.'

I have thought long and hard about this and I have concluded that much of the impact of intergenerational trauma gets deftly – or so they think – covered up by courtesy and good food and that is how it is perpetuated. Then, those who continue to tell lies, or not tell truths, are changed, and hardened.

Let me explain all this and then suggest how I think we can begin to heal. And the horrid giant dolls in their elegant diorama will need more gloss.

Sometimes love has gone. Sometimes it can be nurtured or repaired, but ONLY if there is dialogue, a willingness to look at one another's pain and, the most demanding thing of all, accept and voice that you were the source of it. The latter can only occur in the most loving family home, where an individual is truly loved. We might not like to think of it, but a family, however loving, may not be adequate to their child's needs if, for example, those needs are complex. In trying to respond to needs, a dance begins and, sometimes, much damage is done. We will come back to all of this.

In my family home, when The Mother would punch and pull

my hair, she would sometimes add that I did not understand violence, but that *she* did, because she grew up with it. To this day, no element of that has been discussed. How, you might ask, can witnessing worse violence make it acceptable to perpetuate slightly less on your own child? Then, in a process of attrition born of your own pain, how is it acceptable to gaslight and belittle your own child, feed it out into the world, calling aloud, '*Oh*, what the child might have been, how much better, such a palpable failure,' and feed it back to the child with agreement from the world. How right you were; she is a terrible child, and everyone knows. From aunts, to grandma, to teachers to the dentist and all the things he said about you. This is where trauma can lead you. Into spite. At some point, we must make the decision that, wherever the trauma started, it ought to stop with us: our children deserve better. This is by no means a painless process and it took me decades to understand that there could be change.

It was confusing. I could not accept that the fault could be with a good family who everyone told me was good, so I turned the pain in on myself. Materially, I was well cared for. My parents came from large rural working-class families and ascended to the middle class, by graft and reading. Looking back, they prized material things. I felt guilty for existing and was confused by material care in the absence of other kinds.

There would be such a splendid lunch. That was the odd thing: lovingly grown vegetables, topside of beef and billowing Yorkshire puddings that gave credence to Mother and Father's pronouncements. The Mother, ladling out the best gravy and sweet carrots. It had to be me, didn't it? I was the smut, the little canker on the pod, on the silken corn husk. In my dreams, the corn smut was huitlacoche, which they eat in Mexico as a delicacy. I read about it as I read about everything I could. There, I was prized and devilled up with ancho chillies. There, in the markets, I was as startling and free as Frida Kahlo: I was delicious. But that was only a dream. At home I was neither beautiful nor a dish to covet. You would spit me out.

So those thoughts drove me into the bathroom as a child (post broad bean pudding and leek thinning) when I began to hate myself, all in a rush like a skull thump, and in I would go with a laugh and mock a spit. Then, I would hit my head with my fists, as hard as I could and until my ears were ringing and the passionate beat of my heart and pulse let me feel less alone. Calmed, I would venture out alone and ask if I should help with tea or tidy the shed.

I can tell you that, over the years, I have experienced delirium over pickles, torments over toffees, cabbage, gooseberries, spotted dick, rhubarb crumble and English mustard to go with roast beef. It's a ghastly nostalgia and I must break free of these associations, of lovely meals being a memory. I believe that if I'd had help in my early life, I would not be so sensitised now to smell and texture, rushing me back to beautiful meals and hatred and while I ate them, beautiful birthday cakes and bacon and eggs just so, a thin, dry voice spoke to a little girl. She was me and I was so, so scared.

All that from pain; the ghastly moments with a doll tableau all from pain. Things not spoken of, hurts, lives wasted, unhappy marriages: on it goes, handed down. The dolls replace, for someone, the real people because they can be settled and arranged how you would like. The story goes on to describe how the owner of the dolls cried and crooned over them, *my pretty babies, oh oh oh*. All of this really happened, and I know that I sat there thinking I could not possibly be hearing or seeing any of it. Prizing the doll more than the child. That's *batshit*. It's deranged. And yet we can look carefully and see how a loving person, grown sour and no-one stopping the rot, can end up like that and my heart, well, it melts.

Yes – even to this crazy dance.

It can stop: if there is honesty, conversation, wailing and empathy and rage. If we can see how ragged we are as human beings and what we crack and smash up. We all do it, even the best of us. What eviscerating bad faith to think otherwise and, instead, to sit simmering and lashing out, all smiles, beside your doll tableau or your topside of roast beef.

It *must* stop.

Just fucking stop it – all of it.

7. ON THE EROTIC - IT'S NOT WHAT YOU SEE, BUT WHAT YOU DON'T, AND IT'S RARELY SOMATIC.

'Afterwards, she examined the apartment, opened the drawers of the tables, combed her hair with his comb, and looked at herself in his shaving-glass. Often, she even put between her teeth the big pipe that lay on the table by the bed, amongst lemons and pieces of sugar near a bottle of water.'
— Gustave Flaubert, *Madame Bovary*, chapter nine

The erotic is what you don't see but can think about. It's something half glimpsed: it's texture and thought and tantalising stuff. It's your body and what you do with it in delicate and bold moments, but largely it's intellect and jokes and suggestions.

Here, in the passage from *Madame Bovary*, the delectable bit, the punctum recalling Roland Barthes in Camera Lucida, is the word 'Afterwards,' its resonance deriving from what is not said.

The thing it took me *years* to understand was that the erotic, like romance, need not be about freshness and the new. It can occur, if you keep your wits alive, in old love and in familiarity and this is a wonderful thing. It is an unexpected fuck against a wall, (I do have long-married friends who have a 'sex night' in their diary), but much of it is languorous thought and daydream, into which you have soothed by something from the corner of an eye, unexpected humour, or bravery of some kind. Rebellion, even rage.

Also, silence.

And what was in a place but is not now; as in Keats's 'The Eve of St Agnes', with Porphyro spying on Madeline.

'...and so entranced,
Porphyro gaz'd upon her empty dress
And listen'd to her breathing, if it chanced
To wake into a slumberous tenderness;'

And not too much intimacy, trying too hard to understand oneself or the other becomes tiresome, intrusive, even.

To me, there is misunderstanding. What is pretty might be puffed up, stylish, shiny, unlined, in finery. A highlighted upper lip, a gleam from unguents. Erotic, though? I would say not. Instead, suggestion. Mess. A downy upper lip, a faltering body. It's not ableist, desire; it doesn't see restriction as less, but as only different - or the same. 'Perfection', as the poet Stevie Smith once said, 'is not interesting.' What *is* interesting? Fire in an eye, however tired. A sense of the other's will and rage; of steel and the absurd. Of abundant suggestion. Complicity of the good kind: *make mischief with me.* Or, *I want to take you on.*

I want to take you on.

Maybe.

8. ON QUEERNESS - ON BEIGE AND THE PINK WAFER BISCUIT OF HETEROSEXUALITY.

I have always found heterosexuality a bit strange. A bit sort of beige. A bit dry and thin. Or, say you had a biscuit selection: it's the pink wafer. You know the one: Barbie-pink, made of cardboard and air. I don't get it. That is not to say I would not admit anyone their sexual preferences, more that I cannot feel why you would not wish for and long for plurality.

Which is one way of saying that I am queer. I do not have any particular way of defining it either; I have been married to a man for a long time and it is my design that I will always be married to The Man and if he were to die before me, then any of this would be irrelevant because the likely outcome is that I would get a dog and an allotment. I cannot imagine I would go looking for another partner because he would always be with me.

So, what did it mean and what does it mean now? It is love, admiration, identity. I fancy all kinds of folk and however they identify, and I take pleasure in being able to say I am one thing, I have changed what I am, I may change again, I want none of it, I am sure, well, I think the continuum is important and glorious.

I thought I might marry a beautiful girl, all red hair, and hands red, too, from lambing, or a burlesque dancer, or a wrestler. I suppose I always saw someone feisty and practical and, perhaps, agricultural because there is something very alluring in a hot shepherdess, a woman who can wrestle a sheep and shear quickly and efficiently, oh so many things. I thought usually of buxom women and always with tumbles of curls, jokes, flagrancy, lashings of good food. Broken women, those who cried like me, messy and loving, and unafraid of the ripples and undulations of their flesh. I thought if I married a man - for some reason I had always thought

I would get married - he would be the male equivalent of this. I hoped he would be Welsh, or a hot priest from anywhere at all or a man who could do dry stone walling and cars and man things and then I laughed at myself for being so gendered, so terribly 1950s. But then I forgave myself when I thought of someone wan and poetic with messed-up kajal eyes and a bedhead. And a bed that was never made because there was never time.

When I think, in reveries, when the mind wanders, it is in moods, atmospheres, and I notice it is not even gendered, but entirely fluid, protean, like Milton's angels.

I have been married for twenty-five years to The Man who, as far as I know, thinks and feels very differently from me. That matters not a jot. What we have is just the colour and tenor of our household; it is not infidelity or another not being enough. No. It is history, shared and unshared, colourful thought and mood. And difference.

Beige. I know some things *must* be beige just as some things have to be taupe or builder's magnolia. But only some things, please? Ach, it's dull. There are few things beiger than a heteronormative world. I do not think I understood it existed until it was instilled in me. And the pink wafer biscuit? Barbie pink: surely that is a vibrant and spirited little biscuit. Oh, but it misleads: your pink wafer is made of air and polystyrene, it barely exists. Like beige. I expect you can offer much better analogies, but I would like to recklessly suggest that queer people are more talented at such corollaries. It's because they have more imagination.

9. WHEN LOVE ENDS - FRIENDSHIP, REVENGE, ESTRANGEMENT, THE OTHER

By the time I was an adult, I'd lost both parents, all grandparents, my oldest friend, and the only person in the world with whom I felt safe, my godmother. There was someone called The Other, much older than me. I loved them passionately but was also scared of them and struggled to articulate why. Three years after The Mother died, The Other disappeared. Refused all communication with me and did not explain why. This continued for many years and I experienced it as shame and bewilderment. I felt sick when I thought of it all, still do. I would hear, third hand or so, that The Other wanted nothing to do with me because of what a terrible person I was, because of how badly I had treated my parents (I had done my best to nurse them, I hoped, puncturing any sense of a carefree childhood, bisecting my adolescence or university career, where I felt separate and strange).

Later, I felt the story shift a little within the family, I suppose because the new narrative was easier for people to understand, or more palatable. There had been issues between us: an argument. Yes, that was what had happened. It's the revisionist version of family history. I had tried, before, to raise with my extended family, the matter of events and their impact and, also, of the dark and distressing things which had happened within the family home. The things which led, in part – I am careful to qualify that – to multiple episodes of anxiety and depression. To this day, I still have nightmares about my experience. Some of these nightmares are about The Other. And when I raised these things, emboldened by finally finding the right therapeutic support, I was told, 'If ANY of this had happened, I would have known.' I did not revisit the discussion because I did not want to cause an upset. I could cope and it could have been worse, I reasoned.

When I was about to get married, I tried again to contact The Other: I wanted them at my wedding. Wanted them to know, thought they might want to. This time, I had a reply and it left me on the floor – it was all curses and how I was selfish and hadn't given enough notice: *typical of you*. While I lay on the floor, I thought... well I thought that I would not survive it. I believed – and right here was further endorsement – that I was this terrible person. I had always been told I was, for as long as I could remember. I didn't know otherwise and could not really understand why The Man downstairs wanted to marry me. Still, revisionism came into play: they are upset because you didn't ask them to give you away. That is the accepted version of events, which ignores a decade of refused contact prior to this. Perhaps I did the wrong thing, and I cannot ever have been blameless, but it hurts to have your life described as something you do not recognise. When you've worked out it is a lie, mind you. It can be terribly hard to see clearly.

I had three children. Sent pictures. Nothing. Well, one little thing, once, out of the blue with the first child: 'Thank you for your photograph. I will put it in an album. Regards.' Nothing subsequent. The first baby is now an adult But I kept the note. I'm not sure why. After all, estrangement was their right.

I really struggled with it all because, as I have shown you, I was not raised to think well of myself. I feel uneasy remembering events now and I feel discomfort around my diaphragm and then in my throat. It's the recasting of a story, as if I had somehow withheld them. *My children.* My parents used to do this to me in the *You have Let us Down and You are Here Under Sufferance* lines, where I was the cause of all illness. They had never met them, but it was made plain to me that I ought to have tried harder to introduce them: it was, I was told, what the children deserved.

The Other rang me and said they would be calling at our house. This was one of the most difficult experiences of my life. They told me what I was to do and were explicit that the only reason for visiting was so their wife-to-be knew who I was. I rang a couple of relatives and said that I did not want this, that it was not real, but was told not to behave badly and *I had* to do what my parents would have wanted. They stayed an hour. We lined the boys up for them. They barely spoke to me, talked about work in a sort of boasting way – they are very wealthy from what I can gather – and left. Thereafter, I had further 'precious boys' letters. Tenners on a birthday. Then they dropped the letters, then the treats, then the birthday cards. It took a year for The Other to get bored.

We had a raft of family bereavements. The Other was leading the funeral procession, Looking through me. It felt like a fantasy – as if nothing made sense. In addition to being transparent – they were looking right through me - I felt, as I have on many occasions, like my life was being stolen, my narrative rewritten. On hearing gushing compliments about The Other, on this occasion and others, what I felt was anger and shame. I am still getting over it, but I must accept that people may propel themselves into the heart of my family, and that is that. There is nothing I can say.

I can say one thing to you, though: keeping the peace is also part of intergenerational trauma. It permits terrible behaviour, short-circuits essential conversation. It might look like peace, but no: it is violence.

Without the support of The Man and the one little enclave within my extended family...well thank you. I talk to my friends, too, about bubbles that come up – at children's parties, in the school holidays – family stuff. I can feel like a social leper. But sensible friends now know to jolt me out of this. *It is what it is.* Also, I have The Man and my boys in front of me. It serves me well to have someone remind me not to be ungrateful or self-indulgent. And I do believe that family is a flexible construct and can be built, that our friends and our community are part of it. And that's me, the chubby toddler with a bucket. For years I could not look at pictures of myself for loathing. I'm getting better because there I am.

When I wrote my first book, a semi-autobiographical novel, I drew on homework I had to do in therapeutic support. I had a crisis – breakdown if you like –and received extended support CAT under the NHS with people who saved my life. The Other reappeared just at the end of this support, so I was able to talk it over a little, but not enough, perhaps. In CAT – cognitive analytic (or analytical) therapy – I was asked to write some letters, and the one that follows shortly is instructive.

If something that makes you terribly sad has happened in your family, then your story belongs to you. No-one can steal your life. You were there and you can heal or, more realistically, learn to live alongside bereavement or loss of such a painful, contorted sort. *Yes, you were there. Tell your own story, make your own revisions, if you like, for your own sake, for the sake of your future happiness, but also so that you do not admit impediment to the love you give to others.*

So, here's the letter, as I gave it to the NHS. I should explain that there are references to real people in the letter and, yes, I really did have Albert Camus as my imaginary friend! What can I say: I was and remain a total weirdo. What of it? And obviously clever French men are always sexy. Everyone knows that.

When I was a child, I idolised you. You were like a more fun version of a father, and I would sit on your lap and watch telly or just chat. You spoiled me with sweeties, long walks, playing badminton. I don't remember having a sense of discomfort about my relationship with you as a child. You would joke with my friends and always come to help entertain my friends at birthday parties, but I do have a memory of fearing something and I don't know or cannot articulate what exactly. It came from the corner of your yellow eye. I know that when I was about ten, something changed – or maybe it was always there but I didn't see it until I became more, shall we say, sentient I remember what I thought – or rather willed myself to think – were happy visits, day trips. But they were punctuated by anger, weren't they? You said I was the apple of your eye and that I would always be your precious little girl. But there would be the sudden wild anger, exuberance then angry tears, and I didn't understand. Were you so sad, too? One day, you made the peculiar statement I didn't know whether to admire or run from. You stopped in the street and said, 'I enjoy being a bit of a bastard and kicking people when they are down' and you were all swagger and brilliance. You said, 'People are all shit. It is the nature of the beast. You can't trust anyone, and no-one will care for you' and you smiled knowingly as you said it.

I clung to The Wind in the Willows, *incongruous in your bedroom.* Tits. Being a bastard is fun. Readers' wives. It is the nature of the beast. Cunts. No-one will care for you. All people are bastards. Bestial. It is the nature of the beast. None of this cares for you. Oh, my precious, precious little thing. Raaarrrrrr!

I thought, what beast? What nature? Where is the evidence? Is this something clever people know, or those older and more experienced than I?

I dream of you sometimes, but, for me, it's hard, because my waking and dreaming and my real and imagined encounters are historically a little blurred, but I do not cry to dream again when I dream of you. Instead, I wake and cry not to and I'm a lucky girl now because I reach for the hand of The Man and what can you do to me now?

That is the sad thing, of course: I still get scared because you could

51

appear, as others, like The Mother, and say things and look at me with a cold eye and I would be devastated. It's like you could kill me with a fulsome and triumphant gleam in a cold eye. Me, worthless me, Despicable I: I am dead of shame.

Once, Wales, home in our bisected lives, we went for a walk on the beach. Took a young cousin. He was a lippy sod, but very little and his cheek was funny. But to tell him off, you threw this fully clothed little boy into the freshwater stream running down from shingle to sea. Hard compacted sand. Kid too startled to cry. 'And THAT'S what you get,' you said. How? Why?

I did not know what to do.

You hurt a child.

The child laughed but the child was hurt.

I said nothing more because I had been trained to say nothing, not to trust my own judgement and later I was ashamed, because it was a child, and it was desperately wrong.

The sand was hard, compact, the child was in wet clothes, soaked through in layers.

I am angry now, but then I never felt cross. I just felt sad and dug my nails into the palms of my hands. It was things such as this, I think, that made a place for self-harming to start. I felt a kind of rage and frustration and, as I grew, disgust at my own body: emerging breasts and all. I recall being thirteen and accidentally bumping a drawer on the wall of a bedroom in your house: it made a mark. You were incandescent with rage. I ran out into the street, somewhere, anywhere. In darkness I came back to stern silent looks. When we left you said, 'Next time don't bring her – that – with you.' I hadn't meant to cause harm or damage. 'You marked their wall. You marked it. It was you, you, you. And you are marked, too!' Then, everyone just told me again how selfish I was and, well, the world at large knew that. I felt desperate and just wanted to know if anyone thought differently:

it sounds so pathetic! I said, 'But their next-door neighbours said I was lovely,' and I remember that The Mother barked out a laugh and spat, 'That's because they don't really know you.' I cried silently for two hundred miles home. Mother threw a carton of orange juice, a 'Club' biscuit, and a bag of crisps into the back seat at some point. Like a bone to the nasty little dog. They did not turn around.

What you said – about us always being together, about you and me having adventures together, taking on the world – I thought it was possible. I thought that with your thoughts and words you could make a star dance or melt its heart. Really, your words were hollow – beating on a raggedy old drum. I just didn't know it yet or I tried not to know it. And what you seemed to be was just a layer covering up resentments, wounds and imagined slights: misogyny, pornography, repression, alcohol. And then again, say I do see you, expert on pulling the wool, on subterfuge, on being out in the cold, injured one, turning up to caress a hearse or wear a mourning suit with gravitas, well I won't see you. Can I help with this fiendish task? This morbidity? Can I help? I am important, oh so so so. You don't exist anymore in my head even while you continue to take from me and snarl at me. I wish you only happiness, no harm. I wish you joy and love.'

Do you (reader) think me awful? In a way, I must be, or I cannot function. That is, we are often counselled to forgive to be able to move on: to have closure. I desist. I do not hate, but I do not forgive. It does not embitter me or drive me to be callous with others and it does not constrict my heart. I know that can happen and little is clear in this peculiar world, but I am sure that we make a choice when we are hurt. Will our hearts expand, or will they constrict? That clarity achieved, it is not incumbent on us to forgive, just not to be consumed. You can also be kind, be decent to someone, but not place the pressure, burden even, of forgiveness on yourself.

I am going to say a stark thing and say it through the lens of motherhood. I would throw myself in front of a speeding car to save one of my children; I would probably do it for yours too. I think fondly of my parents if I can place them in moments of warmth and light – and sometimes I cry and think I miss them. There are sensations, happy moments, a lovely garden, the sea and kindness; books, good food and the encouragement to be creative. But really, they are shadowy figures and when I cry – and I do; a lot[5] – I cry not for the idea of missing those I loved, but for the idea of it. That's a significant distinction. I do not feel love, but loss for the idea of love. To put it another way, it is not love, but a picture of it. It took me a long time to understand this, and, in my case, it was my feelings for my children which clarified it.

Love is no longer there. Just a shadow, an echo, and a longing for something that, as far as I can ascertain through layers of memory, was not and might have been. It is sad to think this, but it is honest. Love has ended. On the day The Mother was buried, my father's relatives approached me, and an aunt said, bluntly, 'We won't be seeing you again now, then.' This was a terrible shock, but in a way, perhaps she did me a favour. It was cruel, but in her mind, she was being honest and needed me to know. They were not going to maintain a relationship with family members that, in the end, they did not love, and the youngest aunt was made a spokesperson for the rest. I was twenty. I did not know who to tell, or if this was some sort of psychological emergency. Ought I to have told the vicar? Said, *Help*? On this occasion, what would have been the point? I think it taught me a lesson. Some people prize honesty above all other things and will not pretend when it comes to family relationships or dynamics. Having lost both parents, I lost a whole side of one family, and I have not seen them to this date. They had made a consensus which was, when The Mother had gone, I would be dropped and needed to be told.

I remember feeling the urge to punch, kick and cry but instead I just said to myself, 'One day, I will construct so much more of my own,' and that is what I tried to do. Many mistakes along the way, but I did it. Love was not there, maybe not ever there and I felt sad but, in the end, admitted that what we had was custom and shared experience, but even that, not in depth. It was a pretty thing, a shallow thing, made of necessity and manners and duty.

Love ends. It can with anyone. Sibling, partner, parents, friendships, The Other. What of the love, or what I had thought was love? It broke, then reassembled and went on to light someone else's way. I don't like to think of love dying, purely because it is such a fine thing. Instead, I see it as a glow-worm, and I lost it. Or rather, never really had it. But someone else gained that light, that fine glimmer or burst.

No person is just one thing. That is, if they don't love you and you don't love them, they may still find and give that love. I could say, *Fuck me, you devils, you don't deserve it*, but love is not, *ever*, a matter of deserving. It is pure gift and gifts may be given to the worst of us and that is just how it is.

10. ON LOVE AND HOPE - THE BEST THAT WE HAVE.

'...as if the fullness of the soul did not sometimes overflow in the emptiest metaphors, since no one can ever give the exact measure of his needs, nor of his conceptions, nor of his sorrows; and since human speech is like a cracked tin kettle, on which we hammer out tunes to make bears dance when we long to melt the stars.'
— Gustave Flaubert, *Madame Bovary*, Chapter 12

It is these lines from *Madame Bovary* which give us the title of these essays and we shall return here towards the end of this one. First, let me share lines from one of my own novels, *The Zebra and Lord Jones*. I think they will prove instructive.

At the heart of this novel is a love story between (apparent) opposites. One comes from a rural working-class family, as my own family did, another from suburban gentry. Both have been unloved, but Anwen, the former, is entirely aware of what is missing and entirely aware of her capacity to offer it, nonetheless. Lord Jones, the latter, only knows what love is not. He only knows love in terms of its being missing and his heart is parched. And yet and yet. Anwen is a force of nature, exceptionally intelligent and lucid to the point of its being painful. When Lord Jones meets this, he is aware that he is encountering something new and the novel is, at least in part, about the influence that a full heart – a miraculous survival, in context – may have on an empty one. She is also, against her will, in love with Lord Jones.

'Anwen stopped and stared down the stretches and bends of the Cleddau. She was angry, in awe at this world, full of bitterness at those who had repeatedly shown her what love was not – and full of love for this man.'

In writing that, and in writing the novel, I show you Anwen, mired in trauma, in intergenerational trauma, but able to sit with it and regard it with righteous anger. Magical Realism as a genre sits well for the novel, because it gives full vent to the ways in which our view of the world may be altered by the terrible things which have happened to us, but also how we bring our imagination to bear on that world. Anwen, like me in fact, sees the world tilt; she believes that magic as well as despair is resplendent in the landscape, sometimes seen from the corner or her eye and sometimes felt with a full gaze, meeting her where she is, as here, with an area of the Daugleddau estuary in Pembrokeshire South-West Wales. She is angry, she is bitter, and deservedly so, but because she sees clearly, is intimate with incredible things and 'in awe at this world,' she is lifted up and able to feel so much that is fine. Anwen can be open to all the world offers – she is primed to give and take love and to be of immoderate desire. To me, this is an intensely hopeful way of seeing and being in the world. I mentioned being in love against her will, too. Anwen has a will of iron but, ultimately, will assent when prompted enough.

What of the titular Lord Jones? He knows less than Anwen, as she is keen to point out, strictures of class notwithstanding. Here, though, we see him thinking about a thing he does not understand: love. But he knows what it is not, a refrain in the novel - that sometimes we access the glorious thing, the magical thing, by knowing its opposite. Where we meet him here, he is in a moment of perplexed stillness and he does not understand what is running through his mind; the wonder of the place, the train of liberations it sets in motion for him, and that Anwen's impact on him, her strangeness, confidence, arresting openness, are prompting him to engage with his thoughts, good and bad, and with the world more broadly. He is beginning to open: to sensations in the world, the shifting light on the water with the moonlight, its tidal shifts, and to her. Again, I am describing possibility. Change. Love. Abiding love.

'He knew there was a thing called love, because people talked about it, but he had never connected it with himself, and as we said, he knew from his parents what love was not, while his progress was only through being proper, fine rooms and tellings-off from the column of astringent tweed that was his mother. Oh God, why was he thinking about this nonsense now? Blue light from the water? Shadows from the trees fringing the old quarry?

This strange woman. He had seen her before, of course, but not quite like this. And from his lonely heart came three things: a hatred of what he was and what his were, a deep sadness that pricked at his eyes and a feeling that nothing was ever sweeter than the smell of the soap on the milk jug.'[6]

In the last part of the extract, his senses are more alive and there it is: the erotic in a salty, muddy recess of a place. A tiny observation: the smell of the soap from her hands on the milk jug. She is socially two classes below him, as my grandparents – Anwen is a fictionalised version of my great-grandmother – would have been for some of the people they worked for. She is also above him in any other way: alive to the world, possessed of clarity of thought, of purpose, joyous, and with a burning intellect that could never be disinherited by the rigours of her life. She is also his teacher, the person who takes him away from his cold world – a world of vast privilege, for sure, but also a world of emotional sterility – and into a hot bed, books, intellect, rebellion, and love of the world. I should like to think of them as equals, but my characters become so real to me and I can hear Anwen Llewelyn disagreeing with that, chuckling that she is superior and this is how it is, bach. The point is, that two radically different people have met, have complemented one another but also each has enabled the needs of the individual:

character and development of mind are not subsumed into a twin-whole, the opposite happens. Together, they are both better in the world and to the world – to those who are desperate, grieving; to the natural world we ravage.

So, love may be awakened and bolstered by another. This book is dedicated to my husband, a man I met, as I told you earlier, quite by chance and most definitely when I was not looking. I cannot explain it, but his voice was one I had always known, familiar, though it did not sound like the voice of anyone I knew or had known and was nothing like mine. Obviously, it's familiar now because, as you are reading this, it is my twenty-fifth wedding anniversary, but he remains a puzzle to me: I do not see how I could have met a stranger I had always known. Moreover, sometimes, in my darker moments, it is as if he should not be here. I was not raised, as you have seen, to think well of myself, so how could he have seen me as something so different? Here is hope, too.

It is not essential to be married, to have children, to have a life partner. Not everyone will have lots of friends and there is nothing wrong with that either. So, I want to say that love, incandescently hopeful love, the best of us, is not necessarily found *here*, but will, I hope, always be found *somewhere* if we dare to be open and to appreciate that miracle is around us.

It might be found in the company of reading and community, in learning from the young, in altruism and unexpected meetings. For me, it kept coming back, after hate, after grief. I found it after finding and then losing church: grace, unexpected friends, and fellow travellers as I came to understand that church need not be a building and Christ is not people, who do not leave their personalities and spites at the door. Love rises up from pain and that is bolstering and truly hopeful: everything is impermanent in this world, and after the deepest pain, you may find it again.

Let me return to the title of this book and the quotation I used here as an epigraph.

'...as if the fullness of the soul did not sometimes overflow in the emptiest metaphors, since no one can ever give the exact measure of his needs, nor of his conceptions, nor of his sorrows; and since human speech is like a cracked tin kettle, on which we hammer out tunes to make bears dance when we long to melt the stars.'

Here is a description of what we would long to do with language, as we sit alongside the limits of what we *have*: it will never be enough. Yet we try and we add to it with nuanced gestures. I suppose that is what I have aimed to do in this little collection! To 'hammer out tunes' and hope that by writing about love in its varied incarnations I might hit home, even if it is the work of a second. I've always hated the way that the last line from Philip Larkin in 'An Arundel Tomb' 'What will survive of us is love' is taken in such bold and definite terms, when our 'almost instinct' and its 'almost true' are, at best, approximation. It is there, too, in the poet's description of the crowds who learn to 'look not read.' They are not decoding what is really there, but lifting and deploying something for their own purposes, their own reassurance; quite prescient of Larkin, really: we have learned to look and not read and so he ends up on posters and fridge magnets as an affirmation. But it's true, love is miracle and the full expression of it in language is beyond us and we can only take faltering steps towards it, towards holding it; we can, perhaps, only hold an inchoate understanding of it. All this is fine.

I want to understand God, said someone to me recently, *or how can I believe in Him*? I was puzzled by that; I would say I wanted to believe in a God I was not capable of understanding because He was boundless. That is how I see love too. We cannot fully express it in words, it is mysterious and extraordinary and yet through it we navigate our way in the world and sometimes it is lost. Old as water and new every day. It is demonised, altered, weaponised, but it can grow again in the most arid terrain, I do believe that. It is there in rain on a window, a beautiful painting, a joyful, uninhibited laugh, and when we have it for someone, we do feel that it is so powerful it can do something prodigious, that it carries heat and power and animates our world.

To return to the dedicatee of this book, I met him and then married him with imprudent haste. Twenty-five years to the day as this book is published, I married The Man. I think that I knew, like Lord Jones, what love was not. I had so much to learn. I had also felt how naming it had allowed me to be broken and controlled. People are complicated and, I think, weaponise emotion because of their own pain. Here was the person who was entirely open to the world and what was in it: gentle and quietly sure of himself. A man of faith. Messy, broken, beautiful. The voice I had always known. I still do not understand it; I am still figuring it all out, but as with the limits of language, so with the limits of comprehension.

Happy Anniversary, my darling.

Happy Anniversary to The Man.

ENDNOTES

1   Down There by the Train by Tom Waits and released on American Recordings, Johnny Cash, 1994.

2   I am working with a psychotherapist who is skilled in managing trauma and it goes hand in hand with EMDR. If you are interested, Bessel Van Der Kolk's *The Body Keeps The Score* (Penguin) has extensive accounts of trauma therapy, including EMDR.

3   From Beckett's 1983 novella *Worstward Ho!* And it wasn't supposed to be motivational. I just find Beckett's bleakness inspiring and always have.

4   Anna Vaught, *Famished* (Influx Press, 2020.)

5   I always remember what Dorothy Rowe says in *Depression. The Way out of your Prison.* (Routledge and Kegan Paul, 1983, reprinted Routledge, 1996, 2003), pp. 288: 'Remember, tears are good for you. Tears wash the eyes.'

6   *The Zebra and Lord Jones* (Renard Press, 2023), pp. 132 and 258.

ACKNOWLEDGEMENTS

To my beautiful boys (who will probably never read this, or at least not until after I am dead - think of the content!), for Aaron Kent at Broken Sleep Books for taking on a peculiar little book, thinking it 'vital', leading the work of beautiful publisher and being a generally good egg and for doing such a thoughtful thing and publishing it on my silver wedding anniversary. Thank you to my editor Roisin Dunnett, to my pals in and out of writing and publishing, and to all for reading. Love, big love.

Most of all, to my darling husband, The Man, Ned Vaught. Thank you for asking me for directions on a flooded street twenty-five years and ten months ago. It's all like a dream, isn't it? But, like Caliban, always, 'I cried to dream again.'

Anna x

LAY OUT YOUR UNREST

www.ingramcontent.com/pod-product-compliance
Lightning Source LLC
Chambersburg PA
CBHW051309250626
47155CB00009B/3501